China's Resource Quest: Securing Access to Natural Resources at Home and Abroad

A Monograph
by
MAJ Chad O. Rambo
U.S. Army

School of Advanced Military Studies
United States Army Command and General Staff College
Fort Leavenworth, Kansas

AY 2011

SCHOOL OF ADVANCED MILITARY STUDIES

MONOGRAPH APPROVAL

MAJ Chad O. Rambo

Title of Monograph: China's Resource Quest: Securing Access to Natural Resources at Home and Abroad

Approved by:

_____   Monograph Director
Daniel G. Cox, PH.D.

_____   Second Reader
Clifford Weinstein, LtCol

_____   Director,
Wayne W. Grigsby, Jr., COL, IN   School of Advanced
                                            Military Studies

_____   Director,
Robert F. Baumann, Ph.D.   Graduate Degree
                                            Programs

Abstract

CHINA'S RESOURCE QUEST: SECURING ACCESS TO NATURAL RESOURCES AT HOME AND ABROAD by MAJ Chad O. Rambo, U.S. Army, 54 pages.

In the past decade, China's urban population and economy have grown dramatically. China realizes it must maintain steady and secure access to natural resources in order to placate its populace and maintain economic growth. This monograph examines Chinese actions to secure access to natural resources at home and abroad and discusses the affect a resource secure China has on the United States.

China has shown that she has developed a comprehensive plan to maximize production of domestic natural resources and ensure access to multiple foreign sources, through internal restructuring, partnerships with foreign energy companies and effective use of all elements of national power. China's growing resource security affects the United States primarily in three ways. First, a resource secure China is difficult to leverage or threaten. Second, since China's resource security depends to a large degree on foreign supply, it will be challenging for the United States to pressure countries with which China has resource ties. Third, China's increasing influence in developing areas will cause the United States to revisit its foreign engagement policies.

Table of Contents

ACRONYMS

bbl/d--Barrels per day

CCP--Communist Party of China

CNOOC--China National Offshore Oil Corporation

CNPC--China National Petroleum Corporation

DRC--Democratic Republic of the Congo

ESPO--East Siberian-Pacific Ocean

EIA--Energy Information Administration

IEA-- International Energy Agency

Km--Kilometer

MCC--Metallurgical Construction Corporation

MONUC--United Nations Mission in the Democratic Republic of Congo

Mtoe--Million Tons of Oil Equivalent

NEA-- National Energy Administration

NEC--National Energy Commission

NDRC--National Development and Reform Commission

NOC--National Oil Companies

PRC--Peoples Republic of China

Sinopec--China Petroleum and Chemical Corporation

SPR--Strategic Petroleum Reserve

Tcf--Trillion cubic feet

UNCLOS--UN Convention on Law of the Sea

UN--United Nations

UNSC--United Nations Security Council

WEP--West East Pipeline

Charts

Illustrations

Introduction

China is an ancient society, which has always seen itself as having a prominent role in the world. This view has increased over the last sixty years as China's population and economy have grown exponentially. In order to placate her civilian population and ensure continued economic growth, China needs access to increasing amounts of natural resources. To this end, China has developed a comprehensive and integrated plan for maximizing production of domestic natural resources and ensuring access to foreign supplies, which contributes to her overall security.

China is blessed with a wealth of natural resources, but domestic capacity is no longer able to meet demand. This has increasingly forced China to seek secure access to foreign supplies. China is no longer resource independent, but she has initiated actions to secure natural resources to ensure her continued security, prominence and growth. China has developed a comprehensive plan to maximize production of domestic natural resources and ensure access to multiple foreign sources, through internal restructuring, partnerships with foreign energy companies and effective use of all elements of national power.

China is the world's most populous country with an estimated 1.3 billion citizens.[1] Since the 1950s, China's population has more than doubled, and it has become increasingly urbanized. Massive urbanization is occurring countrywide and is expected to continue well into the future. "In 1949, the year of the revolution, the number of Chinese cities with a population of more than one million was only five, and those with between 500,000 and one million inhabitants numbered

---

[1] Central Intelligence Agency, "The World Fact Book: China," https://www.cia.gov/library/publications/the-world-factbook/geos/ch.html (accessed July 21, 2010).

just eight. In 2000…those numbers had risen to forty and fifty-three respectively."[2] This urban expansion has led to a dramatic increase in demand for natural resources. Metals are required to build new homes, and oil and coal are needed to fuel the production plants and provide electricity to homes.

Although many Chinese remain at or below poverty level, the overall standard of living has increased in the last several decades. This increased standard of living puts additional pressure on China to acquire natural resources and influences foreign policy. One contemporary writer states that "China's actions abroad are propelled by its need to secure energy, metals, and strategic minerals in order to support the rising living standards of its immense population…"[3] One indicator that the Chinese standard of living has increased is the fact that many are now able to afford automobiles. Current projections are that by 2020, there will be more than 500 million privately owned vehicles in China.[4] This will continue to exacerbate the need for petroleum products. Another major factor driving China's thirst for resources is its ever-expanding industrial base, which exploded into being in the late 1970s under the direction of Deng Xiaoping.

Deng Xiaoping succeeded Mao Zedong as the leader of the Communist Party of China (CCP) in 1978. Deng Xiaoping broke with past interpretations of Chinese Communist ideology and "pioneered "socialism with Chinese characteristics" and Chinese economic reform, also

---

[2] James Kynge, *China ShakesThe World* (London: Phoenix, 2007), 29.

[3] Robert D. Kaplan, "The Geography of Chinese Power: How Far Can Beijing Reach on Land and at Sea?," *Foreign Affairs* 89, no. 3, (May/June 2010): 24.

[4] Kynga, 48.

known as the "socialist market economy," which opened China to the global market."[5] As part of these reforms, Xiaoping sought to modernize the four critical sectors of agriculture, industry, science and technology, and the military. These reforms have improved the standard of living of the Chinese people and made China a major power in today's economy, but they have also increased the requirement for natural resources to a level where China is unable to rely on domestic sources alone.

As China's industry modernized and product output increased, it has found itself unable to meet the high resource demands with solely internal sources. The 'great drain robbery' of 2004 is a humorous illustration of China's inability to meet the demand for metal domestically. In the winter of 2004, several hundred manhole covers were stolen from Taiwan, Chicago, and Scotland, and sold as scrap metal to China.[6] The demand for metal in 2004 was so high that thieves across the world were enticed to steal manhole covers to satiate China's appetite for metal.

China's annual energy consumption has more than doubled from 1.107 million tons to 2.265 million tons in the past decade.[7] This makes China the world's largest energy consumer, though the United States still maintains a higher per capita consumption rate. When China

––––––––––––––––––––––––––

[5] David Zweig, *Internationalizing China: Domestic Interests and Global Linkages* (Ithaca: Cornell University Press, 2002), 1; New World Encyclopedia, "Deng Xiaoping," http://www.newworldencyclopedia.org/entry/Deng_Xiaoping (accessed July 21, 2010).

[6] Kynge, 6.

[7] Jenny Barchfield, "China Bests US as World's Top Energy User," *The Boston Globe*, July 21, 2010, http://www.boston.com/news/science/articles/2010/07/21/china_bests_us_as_worlds_top_energy_user/ (accessed July 21, 2010).

reaches a per capita consumption rate equal to that of the United States in 2000, it will require a total energy input three times that of current world consumption.[8]

Chart 1. China's Projected 2020 Energy Consumption

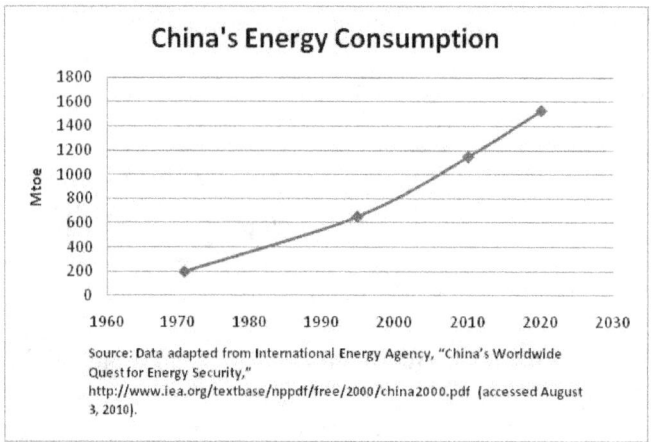

China has attempted to diversify its energy sources in order to mitigate risk and has developed hydroelectric (6%), natural gas (3%), and nuclear (1%) options. However, coal and oil make up the majority of China's energy supply, with coal accounting for 70% and oil for 20%.[9] China is the world's largest consumer of coal, but it is also the world's largest producer.[10] This means coal is a relatively accessible and secure domestic asset.

---

[8] Kynga, 127.

[9] Energy Information Administration, "China Country Analysis," Energy Information Agency, July, 2009, http://www.eia.doe.gov/emeu/cabs/China/Background.html (accessed July 28, 2010): 2.

[10] Ibid., 1.

Chart 2. China's Projected Energy Consumption by Type

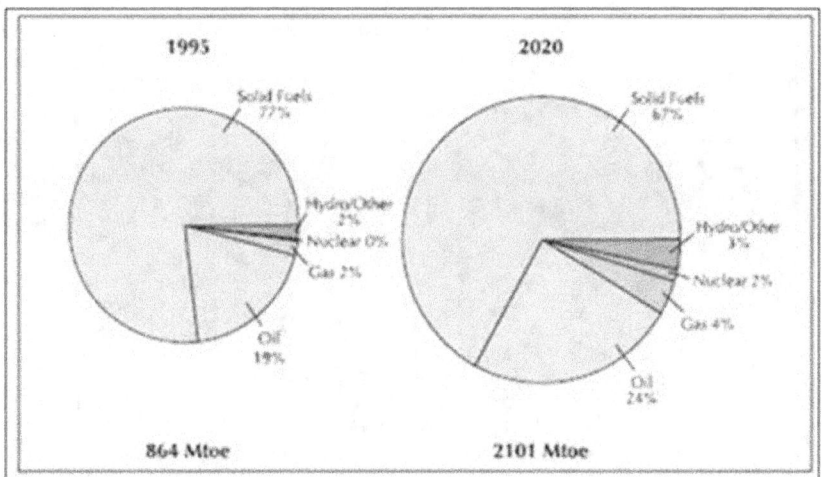

Source: International Energy Agency, "China's Worldwide Quest for Energy Security," http://www.iea.org/textbase/nppdf/free/2000/china2000.pdf (accessed August 3, 2010).

Oil is another matter. China was a net oil exporter as recently as the 1990s, but due to an expanding population and economy, it became the third largest net importer by 2004.[11] China currently requires approximately 8 million barrels per day, but is only capable of producing 4 million barrels per day (bbl/d) domestically.[12] Therefore, China must import the additionally required 4 million barrels per day. Imported oil currently equates to 50% of China's total oil consumption and 10% of her overall energy consumption. China's heavy dependence on imported oil and other natural resources has far-reaching internal security implications. A nation's inability to provide for its own resource needs forces participation in global issues and markets. China views this increased interdependence on others as a threat to its national security and has adopted an approach of seeking diverse sources of supply.

───────────────────────

[11] Ibid.

[12] Ibid., 2.

Chart 3. Chinese Net Oil Imports vs. Domestic Supply

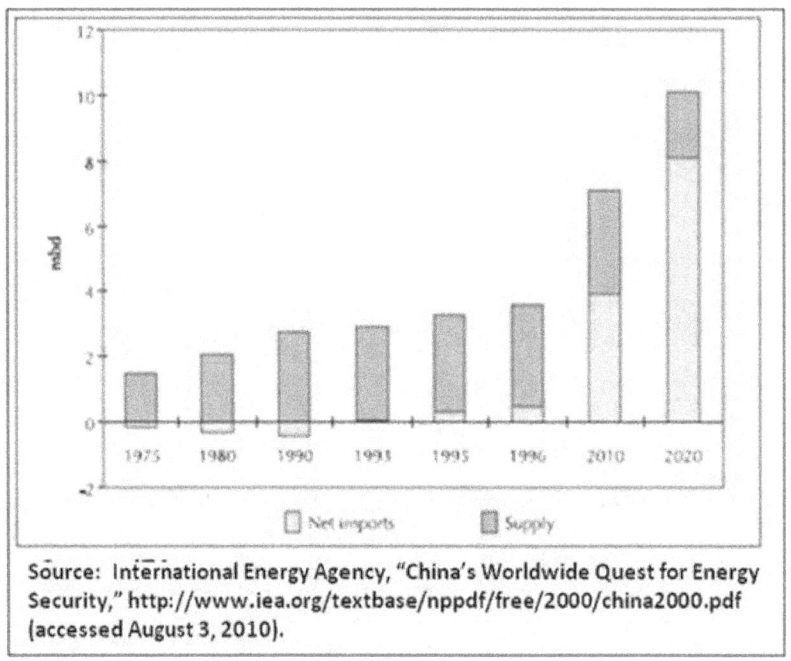

Source: International Energy Agency, "China's Worldwide Quest for Energy Security," http://www.iea.org/textbase/nppdf/free/2000/china2000.pdf (accessed August 3, 2010).

China's ability to establish multiple points of access to resources will have serious implications for the United States. As China becomes more resource secure, the ability of the United States to influence her future actions will diminish. China, with multiple resource options, will be capable of weathering most negative diplomatic or economic actions the United States may levy against her. Thus, increased resource options for China equals decreased influence for the United States.

Chinese resource security will not necessarily lead to conflict with the United States. China understands that by taking part in globalization, she has linked her success to that of the world community. Within this community, stability is essential for economic prosperity.

According to William Overholt, China is our ally in seeking geopolitical security.[13] This is because all "of China's economic successes are associated with liberalization and globalization…"[14] China herself has acknowledged this interdependency with the rest of the world. Chinese Ambassador Zha Peixin has said as much. "In this massive tide of economic globalization, no country can develop and prosper in isolation. China has learnt from her long history that isolation leads to backwardness."[15] Therefore, all indications are that China will continue to compete aggressively with the United States, but she does not seek direct conflict.

China's pragmatic resource policies are often viewed with much angst in the United States. China is not bound by the same moral constraints as the United States in its dealings with foreign countries and therefore has no issue collaborating with fringe states, such as Iran, to achieve her resource needs. This subject poses a significant challenge for United States policy makers in regards to Chinese influence. China continues to partner with Iran and Myanmar, and she has used her position on the United Nations Security Council to protect them against sanctions and other negative actions the United States has tried to implement. The United States will find it more and more difficult in the future to influence the behavior of states like Iran and Myanmar, because China's relationship with these states will only get closer as resources become scarcer. Thus, the United States' influence in the world may decrease with an increase in Chinese resource security.

---

[13] William H Overholt, "China and Globalization," May 19, 2005, http://www.rand.org/pubs/testimonies/2005/RAND_CT244.pdf (accessed September 21, 2010): 4.

[14] Ibid., 1.

[15] Zha Peixin, "China and Globalization," October 10, 2003, http://www.chinese-embassy.org.uk/eng/dsjh/t27161.htm (accessed September 21, 2010).

Structure

This monograph examines the actions China has taken, internally and externally, to secure resources and how resource security for China affects the United States. This monograph is structured into four major sections. The first section provides necessary background information prior to entering the analysis portions. In the background section natural resources will be defined, security theory is discussed with emphasis on energy and resource security, China's resource environment is explored and China's resource policies and energy sector is examined. The remaining sections provide the analysis and synthesis. The second section, examines Chinese domestic capacity and activities to maximize domestic natural resource production and access, as well as security measures to protect these resources. The third section investigates Chinese efforts to gain access to foreign natural resources. Finally, an assessment of China's actions and policies and their implications for the United States are discussed.

Background

Natural Resources

In order to proceed with the investigation into China's actions concerning natural resources, the term 'natural resources' must be defined. This will allow a solid base of understanding throughout the text. Natural resources can be defined in many ways. They can be defined as "a naturally occurring material, e.g. coal or wood, that can be exploited by people" or as "resources occurring in nature that can be used to create wealth."[16] This monograph will only

---

[16] Encarta Online Dictionary, "Natural Resources," http://encarta.msn.com/dictionary_1861696711/natural_resource.html (accessed August 3, 2010); Inestorwords.com, "Natural Resources," http://www.investorwords.com/3210/natural_resources.html (accessed August 3, 2010).

address those natural resources that fuel vehicles, produce energy, or are used in industry. The primary natural resources that meet these requirements are oil, natural gas and other various metals and minerals, such as cobalt, copper and lithium.

Security

The primary goal of any entity is to ensure its own survival. This idea applies equally to states. States may have a multitude of sub-goals and objectives, but these all support the overarching requirement for survival. In order to survive, a state must first see to its security. Security is "the state or feeling of being safe and protected" and a state may employ numerous methods, or combinations of methods, to achieve security.[17] A state can assume an aggressive posture and build up its security sector to such a degree that others are unwilling to challenge it or a state may achieve increased security through collective security or hegemony.

With collective security, states agree to assist in each other's security. Thru alliance, states are collectively better able to secure the peace or deter aggressive nations. The idea of collective security is founded in liberal-internationalism thought. Michael Lind, a liberal-internationalism advocate, believes the world should be organized "as a peaceful global society of sovereign, self-governing peoples, in which the great powers, rather than compete to carve out rival spheres of influence, cooperate to preserve international peace in the face of threats from

---

[17] Encarta Online Dictionary, "Security," http://encarta msn.com/encnet/features/dictionary/DictionaryResults.aspx?lextype=3&search=security (accessed August 3, 2010).

aggressive states and terrorism."[18] In this model, states form alliances to ensure world peace and therefore their own security. The North Atlantic Treaty Organization (NATO) is an example of a collective security organization.

A hegemonic state is an aggressive state that is capable of increasing its security by influencing other states to conduct actions that are favorable to the hegemonic state. This influence can be either positive or negative. According to Niall Ferguson in the

> "world-system theory" of Immanuel Wallerstein,…, "hegemony" means more than mere leadership but less than outright empire. A hegemonic power is "a state ... able to impose its set of rules on the interstate system, and thereby create temporarily a new political order."[19]

John Mearsheimer believes that all mighty states attempt to gain hegemony. His realist theory of international politics states, "that the mightiest states attempt to establish hegemony in their region of the world while making sure that no rival great power dominates another region."[20] By controlling their region of the world and negating the influence of rivals, hegemonic states are able to achieve security. The former Soviet Union's forcing its satellite states (e.g. East Germany) to join the Warsaw Pact is an example of negative hegemonic power.

Robert Kaplan argues that China is taking the hegemonic approach to security.[21] This assertion runs counter to Paul Bolt and Adam Gray's assessment that while China sees itself as a

---

[18] Michael Lind, "For Liberal Internationalism," *The Nation*, (July 2009). http://www.newamerica.net/publications/articles/2007/liberal_internationalism_5538 (accessed November 19, 2010).

[19] Niall Ferguson, "Hegemony or Empire?"*Foreign Affairs* (September/October 2003). http://www.foreignaffairs.com/articles/59200/niall-ferguson/hegemony-or-empire?page=2 (accessed October 14, 2010).

[20] John J. Mearsheimer, "China's Unpeaceful Rise," *Current History* 105, no. 165 (April 2006): 160.

[21] Kaplan, 41.

rising power, it is keenly aware of the dangers associated with becoming a hegemonic power.[22]

Additionally, Stacey Lee states that China's strategy "predominantly favors free riding out of necessity"[23] A nation that is employing a free riding strategy, is either unable or unwilling to become hegemonic. Therefore, China is currently not a true hegemonic state.

If China has not actively sought to enter into collective security agreements or establish hegemony, then what course has she taken? According to a RAND study, China has taken the softer approach of a ""calculative" strategy--that is, a strategy calculated to protect China from external threats as it pursues its geopolitical ascent. The purpose of the calculative strategy is to allow China to continue to reform its economy and thereby acquire comprehensive national power without having to deal with the impediments and distractions of security competition."[24] Qin Yaqing's writings are congruent with the RAND assessment. Doctor Yaqing believes that China is now seeking a peaceful rise in power through cooperative internationalism.[25]

The "calculative" strategy and cooperative internationalism allow China to focus on its economy, versus its military, as a way to obtain security. This is key as "China's grand strategy is perhaps most heavily influenced by its need for consistent, high levels of economic growth" and in "order to maintain its economy, energy security has evolved into a key focus of Chinese

---

[22] Paul J. Bolt and Adam K. Gray, "China's National Security Strategy," United States Air Force Academy, Colorado Springs (2007): 2.

[23] Lee, Stacy L., "China's Energy Security: The Grand "Hedging" Strategy," Monograph, School of Advanced Military Studies, Fort Leavenworth: United States Army Command and General Staff College (2010): 40.

[24] *RAND*, "Interpreting China's Grand Strategy," *RAND,* 2000, http://www.rand.org/pubs/research_briefs/RB61/index1.html (accessed September 14, 2010).

[25] QinYaqing, "China's Security Strategy with a Special Focus on East Asia," http://irchina.org/en/xueren/china/pdf/qyq2.pdf (accessed September 14, 2010): 1-2.

11

national strategy. As long as China's economy sustains high levels of growth, China's energy needs will expand proportionately."[26]

Energy security is a subset of national security and is defined as, "a situation where energy supplies are available at all times in various forms, in sufficient quantities, and at affordable prices."[27] China is no longer able to meet its energy needs solely by utilizing domestic sources. This means that China must supplement its requirements with foreign sources, which increases its overall vulnerability. In an effort to minimize the vulnerability associated with external supply, countries generally develop policies that incorporate the three components of "diversity of supply, reliability of supply to mitigate a single point of failure, and adequacy of supply to meet demand at an "affordable" cost."[28] The International Energy Agency (IEA) describes China's options for ensuring energy security as "developing domestic resources to the maximum possible, creating strategic reserves, seeking foreign technology and investment, establishing reliable and secure oil trading channels, and making strategic investments in upstream production facilities abroad."[29] How China is or is not approaching these options is explored in the following pages.

Geography and Threats to supply

Geography and current security conditions, as they relate to natural resources, have shaped how the Chinese formulate natural resource policy. The principle geographic feature that

---

[26] Bolt and Gray, 4-5.

[27] Lee, 9.

[28] Ibid.

[29] International Energy Agency, "China's Worldwide Quest for Energy Security," 2000, http://www.iea.org/textbase/nppdf/free/2000/china2000.pdf (accessed August 3, 2010).

plays into Chinese external natural resource policy is the Strait of Malacca. The Strait of Malacca, a narrow strait between Singapore and Indonesia, is a major choke point for shipping traveling between the Indian Ocean and the Pacific (See Illustration 1). "The strait is 500 miles (800 km) long and is funnel-shaped, with a width of only 40 miles (65 km) in the south that broadens northward to some 155 miles (250 km) between We Island off Sumatra and the Isthmus of Kra on the mainland."[30] This narrow sea lane lies along the primary shipping route from the Middle East and the Western world to China and the Far East. Though easily interdicted, and at times dangerous, the Strait of Malacca is used to avoid the longer voyage and stormy seas that lay to the south.

Foreign powers or pirates can potentially interdict the flow of resources through the Strait of Malacca, due to the severe canalization. While interdiction is unlikely, it is still a possibility and a strategic concern for China. Concern over the blockage of the Strait of Malacca is a relevant concern, because as recently as 1999 India threatened to close the shipping lane.[31] Piracy is also a perpetual issue in the region. In 2004, piracy near the Strait of Malacca accounted for 40% of piracy worldwide.[32] The Strait of Malacca is an ideal location for pirates, as the terrain on either side of the strait is heavily wooded, with multiple small coves that allow pirates to easily ambush vessels as they transit the strait.[33]

---

[30] Britannica Online Encyclopedia, "Strait of Malacca," http://www.britannica.com/EBchecked/topic/359411/Strait-of-Malacca (accessed August 3, 2010).

[31] Chris Devonshire-Ellis, "China's String of Pearls Strategy," *China Briefing*, March 18, 2009, http://www.china-briefing.com/news/2009/03/18/china%e2%80%99s-string-of-pearls-strategy html (accessed August 3, 2010).

[32] Diana Lee, "Pirates Strike at Will in the Straits of Malacca," *UNIORB*, May 1, 2005, http://uniorb.com/ATREND/piracy htm (accessed August 3, 2010).

[33] Ibid.

Illustration 1. Strait of Malacca and Security of Seaborne Oil Shipments

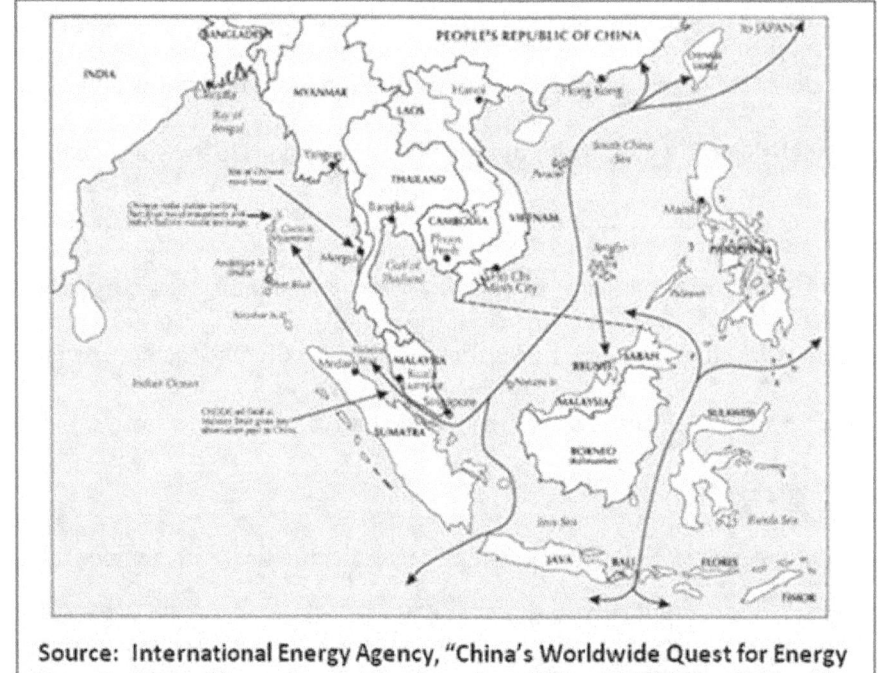

Source: International Energy Agency, "China's Worldwide Quest for Energy Security," http://www.iea.org/textbase/nppdf/free/2000/china2000.pdf (accessed August 3, 2010).

China ratified the UN Convention on Law of the Sea (UNCLOS) and instituted its 'string of pearls' strategy in response to the potential ability of a hostile foreign power to close the Strait of Malacca or pirates to disrupt transit. China has also built the China-Myanmar pipeline as a way to bypass the Strait of Malacca. With the completion of the China-Myanmar pipeline, oil from the Middle East and Africa can be transferred from ships at Myanmar ports and sent through the pipeline to China. By agreeing to abide by the provisions of UNCLOS, China limited some of its potential options, but diminished the chances of foreign nations interdicting its supply. While this action is passive in nature, the 'string of pearls' strategy is active and aggressive. The 'string of pearls' strategy (See Illustration 2) refers to Chinese efforts to secure the vulnerable sea lanes from the Middle East to China by "establishing an increased level of influence along sea routes through investment, port development and diplomacy."[34]

Illustration 2. China's 'String of Pearls'

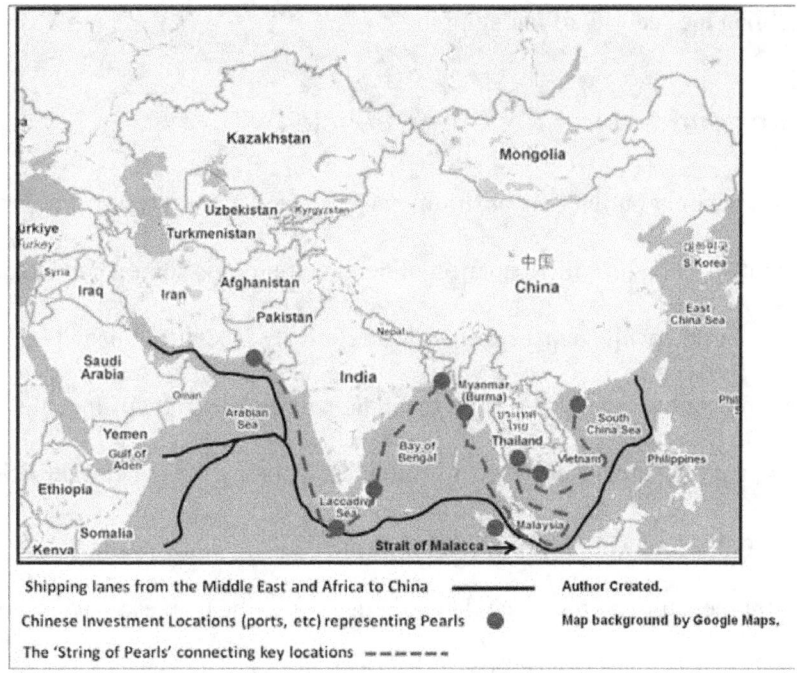

China has taken a comprehensive approach with this strategy and according to Chris Devonshire-Ellis:

> China's investments extend from Hainan Island in the South China Sea, through the littorals of the Straits of Malacca, including port developments in Chittagong in Bangladesh; Sittwe, Coco, Hianggyi, Khaukphyu, Mergui and Zadetkyi Kyun in Myanmar; Laem Chabang in Thailand; and Sihanoukville in Cambodia. They extend across the Indian Ocean, Sri Lanka, the Maldives, Pakistan's Gwadar Port, and in islands within the Arabian Sea and into the Persian Gulf.[35]

---

[34] Chris Devonshire-Ellis, "China's String of Pearls Strategy," *China Briefing*, March 18, 2009, http://www.china-briefing.com/news/2009/03/18/china%e2%80%99s-string-of-pearls-strategy html (accessed August 3, 2010).

[35] Ibid.

As seen in the illustration on the previous page, China has literally established a string of secure sites from China to the Middle East. While the 'string of pearls' does not allow China to truly control the shipping lanes from the Middle East and Africa, it does provide a multi-tiered approach to enabling the security of her shipping.

China's Energy and Natural Resource Policies

China has publicly outlined its position on energy and natural resources through the publication of white papers. Its white paper on mineral resources is somewhat dated, as it was published in 2003, but the white paper on energy is relatively recent (published in 2008). These documents likely do not hold the whole truth to China's resource strategy since they were published openly, but they are nevertheless useful in ascertaining the general direction China is heading. The white paper on energy is broader in its scope than the paper on mineral resources, but both are complimentary and reinforce the main themes of the Chinese government.

The white paper on energy establishes that China's energy development is contingent on the availability of domestic resources and emphasizes thrift, cleanness, and safety as key to energy development.[36] It further expounds on these tenets by stating,

> The basic themes of China's energy strategy are giving priority to thrift, relying on domestic resources, encouraging diverse patterns of development, relying on science and technology, protecting the environment, and increasing international cooperation for mutual benefit. It strives to build a stable, economical, clean and sage energy supply system, so as to support the sustained economic and social development with sustained energy development.[37]

---

[36] "China's Energy Conditions and Policies," 2008, http://www.china.org.cn/e-white/index.htm (accessed July 21, 2010).

[37] Ibid.

As hinted at in the statement above, the Chinese see technological improvements as crucial to improving domestic production. Through scientific innovation, the Chinese look to increase their capability to extract resources in difficult terrain, make the most of available resources and minimize waste. Much of China's untapped resources lie at great depths and in remote areas. These conditions require highly advanced drilling methods and machinery.

China has significantly increased its partnership with foreign energy companies in recent years. This partnership gives China access to a wider array of resource production technologies and expertise. Two areas of focus listed in the white paper on energy were improving external cooperation in the exploration and development of oil and gas resources and encouraging foreign investment in exploration and development of unconventional energy resources.[38] In an effort to gain foreign partnership and investment China issued the *Opinions on Further Encouraging Foreign Investment in Exploring and Exploiting Non-oil-and gas Mineral Resources*. This rather long document established several incentives to foreign companies to operate in China. Particularly it "allows foreign investors, either by themselves or in collaboration with Chinese counterparts, to conduct risk exploration on its territory. Foreign investors who invest in exploring and recovering paragenetic and associated minerals and utilizing tailing or exploring mineral resources in China's western regions are entitled to enjoy the preferential policy of reduction of or exemption from mineral resources compensation fees."[39]

China's white paper on mineral resources also discusses the need for new and innovative means to develop energy as well as the need to work with foreign partners. The white paper

---

[38] Ibid.

[39] Ibid.

17

highlights that in order for China to integrate foreign capacity it has to reform its regulations. The Chinese constitution and the "Mineral Resources Law" of China explicitly state, "mineral resources are owned by the state."[40] While China still maintains ownership of all domestic minerals, it has adjusted its policies concerning mining rights and prospecting to enable and entice foreign investment.

China's Energy Sector

China's current energy sector bureaucracy has undergone several re-organizations over the past decade in an effort to improve resource oversight and policy development. The most recent change occurred in March of 2008, when the National Energy Commission (NEC) and its subordinate National Energy Agency (NEA) were established.[41] The NEC's role is to assist in policy development and conduct intragovernmental energy coordination, while the NEA runs day-to-day operations.[42] The ability of the NEA to manage China's energy sector effectively is questionable. Though nominally subordinate to the NEC (See Chart 4), in reality the National Development and Reform Commission (NDRC) influences NEA operations to a greater extent. This is because the NDRC has direct ties to Chinese Communist Party leadership and provides the National Energy Agency with logistical support.[43] Having two bosses poses a challenge to the National Energy Agency, but their most significant challenge to maintaining effective oversight may be the national oil companies.

---

[40] Ibid.

[41] Erika S. Downs, "China's "New" Energy Administration," *China Business Review* (November/December 2008): 45.

[42] Ibid., 43.

[43] Ibid.

According to Erika Downs, the National Energy Agency:

> Has more political clout than its predecessor but not enough to mitigate the bureaucratic infighting that undermines energy decisionmaking. As a vice-ministerial body, it is a step above the former Energy Bureau, but it still lacks the authority to effectively coordinate the interests of ministries, commissions, and state-owned energy companies. The heads of some of these companies—for example, the CNPC, China Petroleum and Chemical Corp. (Sinopec), State Grid Corp, and Shenhua Group—hold ministerial rank. One complaint of former Energy Bureau officials was that energy companies often undercut Energy Bureau authority by holding face-to-face discussions with senior PRC leadership.[44]

Chart 4. China' Energy Sector

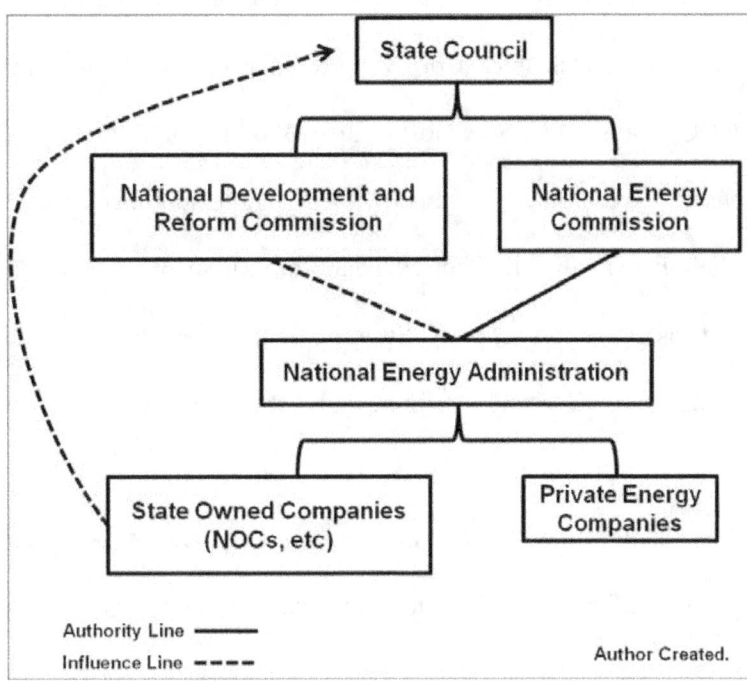

The national oil companies (NOCs) dominate the Chinese energy sector. While the coal and other resource industries are a mix of government and privately owned companies, oil and natural gas are firmly in control of the NOCs. The national oil companies are extremely powerful and influential entities, and as mentioned above, are often able to circumvent notionally higher-

---

[44] Ibid.

level government institutions in pursuit of profits. The national oil companies' ability to act in its own best interest, while attempting to align those interests with government objectives, is illustrated in that they "have ignored guidance from the central government about where they should invest overseas. China National Petroleum Corp. (CNPC) acquired more assets in Sudan even after the National Development and Reform Commission excluded Sudan from a list of countries in which Chinese oil companies were encouraged to invest in 2007."[45]

The three primary national oil companies are China National Petroleum Corporation (CNPC), China Petroleum and Chemical Corporation (Sinopec), and China National Offshore Oil Corporation (CNOOC). The CNPC is the most influential of the three and leads China in upstream development.[46] According to the Energy Information Administration (EIA), "CNPC, along with its publicly-listed arm PetroChina, account for roughly 60 percent and 80 percent of China's total oil and gas output, respectively. Sinopec, on the other hand, has traditionally focused on downstream activities such as refining and distribution with these sectors making up 76 percent of the company's revenues in 2007."[47] China National Offshore Oil Corporation is a newer national oil company and as the name implies, primarily deals with offshore exploration though in recent years it has expanded its refinement capability in order to compete with CNPC and Sinopec.[48]

To increase its resource security China has effectively identified threats to its overseas resource supply routes and has implemented actions to secure those lines. She has also clearly

---

[45] Ibid.

[46] EIA, 3.

[47] Ibid.

[48] Ibid.

outlined her overarching ideas on energy and resources through the publication of white papers. Lastly, China has restructured its energy sector to make the most of the resources it has at home.

China at Home

This section examines China's domestic natural resources and her capability to extract and utilize them. There are four sub-sections: Oil, Coal, Natural Gas, and Security. The first sub-section provides an overview of China's oil reserves and production capacity. The second sub-section addresses China's coal supply and industry. The third sub-section discusses China's increased use of natural gas and natural gas reserves. The last sub-section will briefly discuss current Chinese actions to safeguard domestic natural resources.

Oil

China did not require large amounts of oil until the 1970s when the economy and population began to expand rapidly. This expansion was primarily due to Chinese society shifting from agrarian based to industrial based. Since then production at domestic fields has dramatically increased, with production increasing from approximately half a million barrels a day in the early 1970s to over four million barrels a day in 2008.[49]

---

[49] International Energy Agency, "China's Worldwide Quest for Energy Security," 2000, http://www.iea.org/textbase/nppdf/free/2000/china2000.pdf (accessed August 3, 2010): 22; EIA, 3.

Illustration 3. China's Major Oilfields

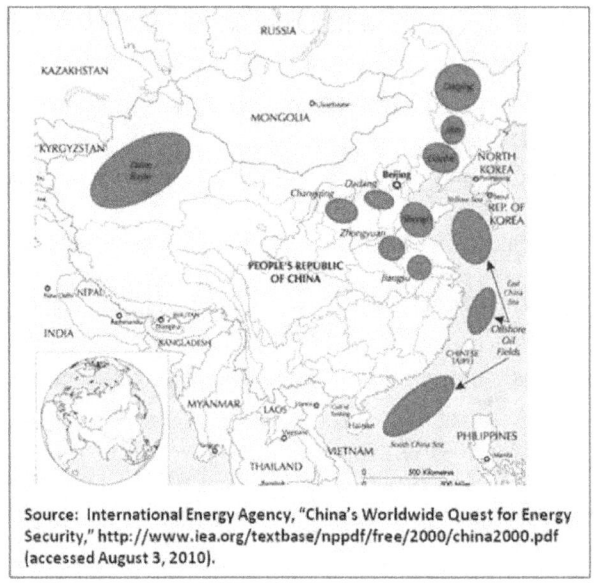

Source: International Energy Agency, "China's Worldwide Quest for Energy
Security," http://www.iea.org/textbase/nppdf/free/2000/china2000.pdf
(accessed August 3, 2010).

Mainland

The vast majority of China's oil reserves are located inland. The oldest oilfields are

located in the northeast portion of the country with the Daqing field being the largest. Daqing was

discovered in 1959 and has been the most significant producer to date, with an annual output

equating to almost one third of China's total domestic oil production.[50] While these northeastern

fields helped fuel China's economic growth, their output is expected to severely decrease in the

near future. Since 2006, the Daqing field has declined from an annual production of 100 million

tons to approximately 40 million tons.[51] As the Daqing, and the other northeastern fields enter the

late stages of production, the efficacy of recovery methods has been a focal point of China. China

---

[50] International Energy Agency, "China's Worldwide Quest for Energy Security," 22.

[51] CNPC, "Daqing Oil Province,"
http://www.cnpc.com.cn/en/aboutcnpc/ourbusinesses/explorationproduction/operatediol/default htm
(accessed September 4, 2010).

has looked to new technology to maximize the amount of recoverable oil from these declining fields.

One method being used is "utilizing natural gas supplies from the Daqing field for reinjection purposes to fuel enhanced oil recovery (EOR) projects."[52] The use of enhanced oil recovery methods may result in maximizing the amount of oil that can be recovered from the northwestern wells, but it also increases the demand for natural gas. Additionally, CNPC has developed and utilized a number of tertiary recovery methods to include foam combination flooding and polymer flooding. These initiatives have resulted in a recovery rate of approximately 50 percent in the Daqing fields.[53]

As the northeastern fields have started to decline in recent years, exploration of inland fields has focused on the Tarim Basin in the Zinjian Uygur Autonomous Region in the northwestern portion of the country. The Tarim Basin includes the main field as well as several smaller fields and has an estimated 78 billion barrels of reserves.[54] These estimates have given hope to the Chinese that they will be able to reduce their import of foreign oil after the Tarim Basin is fully developed.

Development of the Tarim Basin has proven challenging in the remote Xinjiang Province. "Several obstacles impede exploration and development: deep pay zones, high drilling costs, complex geology, high subsurface pressures and temperatures, a harsh climate and a lack of infrastructure in this extremely remote area."[55] Since the 1970s, China has focused its

---

[52] EIA, p4.

[53] "Daqing Oil Province.".

[54] EIA, 4.

[55] International Energy Agency, "China's Worldwide Quest for Energy Security," 24.

infrastructure along the eastern coastal areas. This was because the eastern coastal areas contained the most populous cities and these cities served as the foundation for China's industry and economy. In contrast, Xinjiang Province and other western areas offered little to the Chinese economy until oil and gas were discovered there. As a result, China devoted most of its infrastructure development to the east and neglected the west. This has proven a costly mistake as China is now unable to fully develop its resources in the west due to the inability to access these areas.

China has begun fostering closer relationships with foreign oil companies in an effort to overcome the challenges associated with developing the Tarim Basin:

> China opened sections of the Tarim basin to foreign investment in February 1994. The five blocks up for international bidding covered 72,730 km2, an area larger than the Netherlands and Belgium combined but only about an eighth of the basin's total. Reacting to reports that these blocks are the most difficult to explore and potentially the least profitable, China offered another eight blocks in June 1995 and gave foreign interests access to some of the better blocks in 1997.[56]

After some initial failures, NOCs and foreign companies have increased production by introducing new technology and improving infrastructure in the Tarim Basin. China understands that in order to maximize its potential it must increasingly open its doors to outside assistance. With the improvements in technology and infrastructure, China expects to increase production in the Tarim Basin over the next decade. In 2008, production in the Tarim Basin was approximately 6.45 million tons of crude oil and CNPC aims to more than double that by 2020. This is a lofty goal considering the difficulties associated with the Tarim Basin.

---

[56] Ibid.

24

Offshore

China is also looking offshore for its oil needs. According to the EIA offshore production currently accounts for approximately 15 percent of China's oil supply and this area will see the largest future growth.[57] The areas of most promise include the Bohai Bay, Pearl River Delta, and South China Sea.[58] The CNPC has assessed that new field discoveries in the Bohai Bay could be the most significant in recent history and could account more than 50 percent of total production by 2015.[59] ConocoPhillips is the largest foreign company involved in the Bohai Bay, with other foreign companies, such as Shell, Chevron, and BP, participating in other areas.[60] China has given foreign oil companies much more access to offshore development than on the mainland. China has granted this access in an effort to maximize locating and developing offshore reserves by leveraging foreign technologies.

Refining

Once the crude oil is extracted from mainland or offshore fields, it must be refined into a usable form. As of January 2009, China was operating 53 refineries (Sinopec and CNPC control 85 percent of the refineries in China) with daily capacity of over 6 million barrels.[61] The CNPC continues to expand its capability and recently began construction of a new refinery in Yunnan

---

[57] EIA, 4.

[58] Ibid.

[59] Ibid, 4-5.

[60] Ibid, 5.

[61] EIA, 8.

Provence in September of 2010.[62] This refinery is positioned at the terminus of the China-Myanmar pipeline, and will refine crude oil from Myanmar and overseas suppliers. Small refineries account for the remaining 15 percent of China's refining capability, but this number continues to decrease. China has closed many small refineries in an effort to increase efficiency. These small refineries were originally designed to process light and sweet crude from mainland fields and are not capable of processing offshore oils or foreign oil without major modifications. These modifications include the need for stainless steel equipment to refine high-acid oils from offshore or foreign fields. [63] The Chinese government is unwilling to modernize the less efficient smaller refineries and has focused on building new modern high capacity facilities, which fall under the control of the NOCs.

Reserves

China outlined in its 10th 5-Year Plan (2000-2005) the need to establish a Strategic Petroleum Reserve (SPR). The SPR is part of China's plan to mitigate the vulnerabilities associated with having to rely increasingly on imported oil. According to the EIA, this system:

> Will be built in three stages, and, in 2004, China started construction at four sites that would comprise the first phase of the country's nascent strategic oil reserve program. Phase 1 has a total storage capacity of 103 million barrels at four sites, and was completed in early 2009. Phase 1 storage capacity will amount to approximately 25 days of net oil imports based on 2008 estimates of Chinese oil demand. Phase 1 sites include: Zhenhai in Zhejiang Province (planned capacity 32 million barrels); Aoshan, also in Zhejiang Province (31 million barrels); Huangdao in Shandong Province (20 million barrels); and Dalian in Liaoning Province (19 million barrels). Thereafter, Phase 2, already under construction, is expected to increase capacity to almost 270 million barrels

---

[62] Winnie Zhu, "CNPC Starts Building China Part of Myanmar Pipelines, Yunnan Oil Refinery," *Bloomberg News*, September 12, 2010, http://www.bloomberg.com/news/2010-09-13/cnpc-starts-building-china-part-of-myanmar-pipelines-update1- html (accessed September 14, 2010).

[63] EIA, 8.

by 2011. Ultimately, Phase 3 is expected to bring total strategic oil reserve capacity in China to about 500 million barrels, although there is no timetable set for this plan.[64]

The establishment of a SPR has significantly reduced the risk to China's security. With the completion of Phase 1, China is currently capable of operating for approximately 25 days without re-supply. Phase 2 completion will increase this capacity to approximately 60 days and Phase 3 will allow China to operate without an outside supply for over 100 days. Even with these substantial numbers, some Chinese officials feel that a larger SPR is needed. According to Chen Geng, a member of the National People's Congress, "current state crude reserves are far lower than sufficient."[65] Geng and other parliamentarians are calling for an increase of both refined and crude oil in order to increase China's energy independence and security.[66] The completion of China's SPR will enable China to overcome any low level disruptions, such as piracy along sea-lanes, to its supply and will be a key enabler in the extreme case of war cutting off outside supply.

Coal

Coal is an important national asset for China, as it provides nearly 70 percent of China's energy needs. China accounts for approximately 40 percent of the world's annual coal consumption, making it the world's largest coal consumer, but fortunately China has the world's

---

[64] EIA, 9.

[65] Michael Hoven, "Chinese Legislators Want Increased Strategic Oil Reserves," March 8, 2010, http://www.heatingoil.com/blog/chinese-legislators-want-increased-strategic-oil-reserves308/ (accessed September 16, 2010).

[66] Ibid.

third largest coal reserves, behind the United States and Russia, with an estimated 13 percent of known coal reserves.[67]

Unlike oil and natural gas, which are controlled by the NOCs, China's coal industry is a mix of state owned and private mines. The small state and privately owned mines have been plagued with production problems stemming from inefficient business practices and outdated equipment. China has closed between 20,000 and 50,000 small mines in recent years and focused on large mines in an effort to increase production levels and reform the industry.[68] China's white paper on energy places emphases on investing in and developing new technologies. It states:

> The equipment manufacturing industry is the foundation of the development of energy technologies. China gives impetus to the technological progress of the equipment manufacturing industry through key state projects. The Chinese government encourages the development of comprehensive excavation machinery in coal mining, large comprehensive mining, hoisting, transport and washing equipment for underground coal mining, and heavy-duty open-pit mining machinery. It supports the development of complete sets of large equipment for coal chemicals as well as R&D of coal liquefaction and gasification....[69]

China is aggressively seeking to modernize and reform its coal industry so that the increasing demand for coal can be met by domestic production. Ironically, even though China has huge reserves of coal it has begun to import coal in recent years. The high production and internal transportation costs of domestic coal, due to inefficiencies and infrastructure issues, made importing coal more cost effective.[70] Some estimates foresee China actually becoming a net coal

---

[67] EIA, 13.

[68] Ibid.

[69] "China's Energy Conditions and Policies," 2008, http://www.china.org.cn/e-white/index.htm (accessed July 21, 2010).

[70] EIA, 14.

importer in the next decade.[71] China sees the need to import coal as not only embarrassing, but also a real threat to its energy security. While coal is one of China's greatest resources, it cannot take the place of oil, and its heavy use has led to significant environmental concerns. These environmental concerns have caused China to look to alternative energy, including natural gas.

Natural Gas

Natural gas has not played a significant role in China's development as it accounts for only two to three percent of overall energy consumption. However, in recent years the demand for natural gas has increased. Natural gas in China is primarily utilized in industry and for fertilizer production, but its use in the residential sector has begun to grow.[72] The expansion of natural gas into the residential arena is due to the increasingly high cost of oil and the need to decrease pollution associated with coal. According to the EIA, China "anticipates boosting the share of natural gas as part of total energy consumption to 10 percent by 2020 to alleviate high pollution from the country's heavy coal use."[73]

While natural gas is a cleaner alternative than coal, it faces challenges becoming a major energy source in China. First, China does not have abundant natural gas reserves. Second, the infrastructure needed to supply China's residential areas is not in place. Due to the cost and scale of establishing this infrastructure, it will be several years before natural gas is fully available even within China's larger cities. Second, a significant portion of China's estimated natural gas

---

[71] Ibid.

[72] EIA, 10.

[73] Ibid., 10.

reserves lie in the challenging Tarim Basin area. China's natural gas challenges are outlined in an International Energy Agency study:

> China as a whole is not endowed with abundant gas reserves. Its proven reserves stand at around 1.5 trillion cubic metres (tcm), accounting for less than 1 per cent of the world's total. Its available gas reserves are located far away from demand centres, requiring the construction of long-distance pipelines. Gas prices are relatively high compared to international levels and China does not have any domestic manufacturing capacity for gas turbines or combined-cycle gas turbines (CCGT).[74]

The Tarim Basin is assessed to have approximately 35.3 trillion cubic feet (Tcf) or roughly one half of China's proven natural gas reserves and is the largest producer (22 percent of China's total in 2008).[75] Conditions at Tarim Basin are challenging physically and geographically. The physical environment of rugged hills and lack of road networks has hindered exploration. As of 2009, only 12 percent of the area had been explored for natural gas reserves.[76] The Tarim Basin's location within China has caused distribution issues once the natural gas is found and extracted, because the Tarim Basin is in the far northwestern portion of the country and away from major industrial and distribution hubs.

---

[74] Xavier Chen, "Developing China's Natural Gas Market: The Energy Policy Challenges," *International Energy Agency*, 2002, http://www.iea.org/textbase/nppdf/free/2000/chinagas2002.pdf (accessed September 16, 2010). 19.

[75] EIA, 11.

[76] Ibid.

Illustration 4. China's Natural Gas Reserves (2002)

Source: Xavier Chen, "Developing China's Natural Gas Market: The Energy Policy Challenges," *International Energy Agency*, http://www.iea.org/textbase/nppdf/free/2000/chinagas2002.pdf (accessed September 16, 2010).

In order to bring natural gas from the Tarim Basin to the eastern markets, China built the West-East-Pipeline (WEP). The WEP is a 4,000 kilometer long pipeline that runs the width of the country from the Tarim Basin in the west to Shanghai in the east. Completion of the WEP was a major milestone in China's natural gas expansion, but pipelines remain a limiting factor in the growth of natural gas. China has roughly 16,000 miles of pipeline compared to 300,000 in the United States. This illustrates how far China has to go before natural gas is fully integrated into its energy sector and society as a whole.[77]

---

[77] EIA, 11.

31

Illustration 5. China's Natural Gas Infrastructure

Source: Xavier Chen, "Developing China's Natural Gas Market: The Energy Policy Challenges," *International Energy Agency*, http://www.iea.org/textbase/nppdf/free/2000/chinagas2002.pdf (accessed September 16, 2010).

Offshore natural gas production remains limited, but China has increased exploration and investment in recent years. As with oil, CNOOC controls the largest share of offshore production and is responsible for managing the most significant offshore natural gas field. China National Offshore Oil Corporation (51%) along with British Petroleum (34%) and Kuwait Foreign Petroleum Exploration Company (15%) operate the Yacheng 13-1 field in the South China Sea.[78] Yacheng 13-1 is the largest offshore natural gas field and supplies a large portion of Hong Kong's

_____

[78] Ibid.

power needs.[79] Multiple other fields exist in the South China Sea and Bohai Bay, but they remain low-level producers to date.

Resource Protection

China is extremely concerned with protecting its domestic resources and aggressively pursues anyone it deems as a threat to its energy sector. In March of 2010, an Australian was sentenced to 10 years in prison for attempting to obtain information concerning China's iron ore purchases and in July 2010, China sentenced an American geologist and two Chinese nationals to eight years in prison for allegedly attempting to collect intelligence on China's oil industry.[80] The American geologist was working in China and had attempted to purchase a database with information related to China's oil industry. China considers this information sensitive, and she has used its state secrecy laws to prosecute the group.[81] These instances illustrate how seriously China views protecting its national resources and ensuring its energy security.

China understands that its domestic mainland oil fields are in decline, the Tarim fields are geographically challenging and that its best future source of domestic oil lies offshore. Therefore, she has vigorously pursued advanced technologies and built relationships with foreign energy companies to maximize domestic production and enhance extraction techniques offshore. Additionally, China has sought to mitigate risk to supply by establishing a substantial petroleum reserve. China has also restructured its coal industry to ensure a constant supply of its most robust

---

[79] Ibid.

[80] Kieth B Ritchburg, "China Sentences American Geologist to 8 Years for Stealing State Secrets," *Washington Post*, July 25, 2010, http://www.washingtonpost.com/wp-dyn/content/article/2010/07/05/AR2010070500859.html?hpid=moreheadlines (accessed August 12, 2010).

[81] Ibid.

resource. She has instituted new policies to expand the usage of natural gas and has taken steps to increase the infrastructure needed to move to more natural gas usage. In all of her actions at home, China has aggressively protected any real or perceived threats to her resources. Now that China has set the conditions for success at home, she has set her sights on acquiring natural resources abroad.

China Abroad

Chinese actions to acquire foreign resources are discussed in this section. The section has three sub-sections: Oil, Natural Gas, and Other Significant Natural Resources. Each sub-section will examine where China is seeking foreign resources and how she uses her elements of national power (diplomacy, information, military and economic), to gain access to resources. In some countries, China uses a mix of its elements of national power to achieve its goals, while in others it is able to achieve its goals by employing only one element of national power. The cases examined are not an all-encompassing list of China's foreign resource endeavors. The cases/countries selected highlight some of China's most significant foreign resource activities.

Oil

China imports the majority of its oil from the Middle East and Africa, though Russia is also a major supplier. Between the months of January and May 2009, China imported approximately 1.7 million barrels of oil a day from the Middle East, 870,000 barrels a day from Africa, and 299,000 a day from Russia.[82] Saudi Arabia and Iran are the largest suppliers of Middle Eastern oil to China, and Angola is the largest African supplier (See Chart 5).

---

[82] EIA, 6.

Chart 5. China's Primary Oil Providers

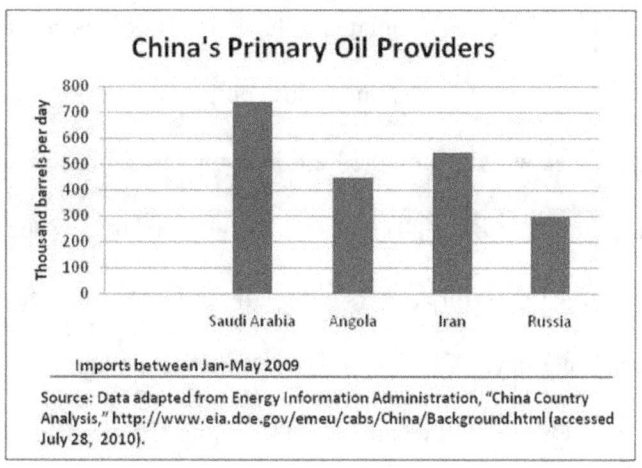

China's Primary Oil Providers

Imports between Jan-May 2009

Source: Data adapted from Energy Information Administration, "China Country Analysis," http://www.eia.doe.gov/emeu/cabs/China/Background.html (accessed July 28, 2010).

Middle East

Saudi Arabia and China continue to maintain positive relations. This is only natural since China is Saudi Arabia's largest oil buyer and Saudi Arabia is China's largest oil provider. Both nations depend on each other for continued economic growth, and the economic arena is where their ties are strongest. While their political agendas sometimes overlap, there has been limited cooperation between the two countries outside the economic sector. The major non-economic venture between China and Saudi Arabia occurred in 1988 when China sold CSS-2 Intermediate Ballistic Missiles and associated equipment to Saudi Arabia.[83] Besides this one instance of military cooperation, China has been able to rely on limited diplomacy to achieve its resource goals associated with Saudi Arabia. This is primarily due to the fact the Saudi Arabia is a wealthy and relatively stable country that does not need anything from China except its continued business.

---

[83] Federation of American Scientists, "Saudi Arabian Missiles," http://www.fas.org/irp/threat/missile/saudi htm (accessed September 30, 2010).

35

China and Iran completed an agreement in December 2007 for Sinopec to develop Iran's Yadavaran oil field. The Yadavaran field is estimated to have 3.2 billion barrels of oil reserves and 2.7 trillion cubic feet of gas reserves, with a maximum output of 300,000 barrels a day.[84] Under the $2 billion deal, Sinopec will develop the field in two phases. Phase 1 will occur over four years (to be complete in approximately 2011) with a daily production of approximately 85,000 barrels per day. Phase 2 will last three years with daily production increasing to approximately 185,000 barrels per day.[85] China and Iran reached several additional energy agreements in the summer of 2009. Under the agreements, various Chinese companies will build seven new refineries, expand two existing refineries and build a 1000 kilometer Trans Irania pipeline.[86]

Angola

Angola is the second largest oil producer in Africa, behind Nigeria, and China's greatest oil supplier and trading partner in Africa. China began building its current relationship with Angola in 1983 when the two established official diplomatic relations. The Chinese-Angolan relationship burgeoned in 2004. At this time, Angola was in search of external support to begin rebuilding after its decades long civil war that ended in 2002. Angola was unable to gain support from international institutions, such as the World Bank, due to transparency and corruption issues

---

[84] Elaine Kurtenbach. "China's Sinopec, Iran Ink Yadavaran Deal." USA Today, December 10, 2007. http://www.usatoday.com/money/economy/2007-12-09-231119728_x htm (accessed September 30, 2010).

[85] Ibid.

[86] Michael Wines, "China's Ties with Iran Complicate Diplomacy," New York Times, September 29, 2009, http://www.nytimes.com/2009/09/30/world/asia/30china.html?_r=1 (accessed October 5, 2010).

and found China to be a willing partner.[87] China, with its non-interference attitude, was willing to offer significant support to the Angolan government in return for access to resources, primarily oil.

In March of 2004 China, through its state owned Export-Import Bank, offered a $2 billion oil-backed loan to Angola.[88] In return for the developmental loan, Angola agreed to provide 10,000 barrels of oil a day to China. Additionally, the agreement stipulated that 70 percent of reconstruction contracts be awarded to Chinese companies, 99 percent of which are state owned.[89] China increased the loan amount by $2.5 billion between 2006 and 2007. This increase included $300 million to rebuild the Benguela railway, which connects Angola to the Democratic Republic of the Congo (DRC), another country with heavy Chinese investment.[90] China's investment of $4.5 billion makes her the largest single investor in Angola's reconstruction effort.[91]

In addition to economic power, China has employed its informational element of national power in Angola to shape the environment to its needs. The information element has been used in an attempt to bring the two cultures closer together and offset some of the Angolan resentment at the fact that Chinese workers have been imported to work on reconstruction projects, thus taking jobs away from locals. The primary way that China is attempting to win the hearts and minds of

---

[87] Kweku Ampiah and Sanusha Naidu, eds., *Crouching Tiger, Hidden Dragon? Africa and China* (Scottsville: University of KwaZulu-Natal Press, 2008), 108.

[88] Ampiah and Naidu, 109.

[89] Ibid., 110,115.

[90] Kent H. Butts and Brent Bankus, "China's Pursuit of Africa's Natural Resources," Center for Strategic Leadership, U.S. Army War College, Carlisle Barracks (2009): 7.

[91] Ampiah and Naidu, 110.

local Angolans is through education. According to Jennifer Parenti, China has initiated a robust information campaign in Africa and is using education to spread its message.

> In the educational forum, Beijing's initiatives include setting up 100 rural schools; providing training for education officials and teachers at all levels; building Confucius Institutes to teach the Chinese language in Africa; establishing government programs to encourage teaching African languages in China; and creating a number of student exchange programs.[92]

China will continue to use information to shape internal and external perceptions of its actions in Angola to maintain access to oil.

China has not employed its military power to a large degree in Angola (as compared to Sudan where China has deployed some 4,500 military personnel to protect oil infrastructure), but this may change in the future.[93] In May of 2010, Francisco Furtado, the Angolan Armed Forces Chief of Staff has hinted that Angola and China may increase military cooperation. "Studies are under way into the re-equipping and the modernisation of our forces, with a view toward cooperation with the armed forces... and the defence industry in China."[94] This announcement could signal that China is preparing to increase not only its arms sales to Angola (China has already provided Angola with SU-27 aircraft and small arms), but will also begin military exchanges and/or bilateral exercises.[95]

----

[92] Jennifer L. Parenti, "China-Africa Relations in the 21st Century," *Joint Forces Quarterly*, issue 52 (1st quarter, 2009): 121-122.

[93] Butts and Bankus, 9.

[94] "Angola Mulls Chinese Military Deals," *AFP*, May 28, 2010, http://www.google.com/hostednews/afp/article/ALeqM5gmU9VQ_xDYErwwsGwR1snJPe4Lug (accessed October 16, 2010).

[95] Butts and Bankus, 9.

China has secured access to resources in Angola through a concerted use of its elements of national power. Diplomacy set the conditions for the employment of economic power (realized through China's state owned enterprises), which has led Chinese action in Angola. As economic efforts continue, so will Chinese information campaigns and potential military relationships. China will continue to leverage all elements of its national power to ensure it is capable of maintaining a steady supply of imported oil from Angola.

Oil Transport to China

Imported oil primarily reaches China by sea. This is because the majority of China's imported oil comes from the Middle East and Africa. Iranian oil also reaches China via shipping. As mentioned earlier, China has long been concerned about the interdiction or disruption of seaborne shipments, especially near the Strait of Malacca. To address this potential problem China has implemented its 'String of Pearls' strategy, as discussed earlier, and pursued pipeline ventures with foreign suppliers.

There are four pipelines currently functioning or in development to connect China to external sources of supply. They are the Kazakhstan-China Pipeline, the East Siberian-Pacific Ocean Spur, the Myanmar-China Pipeline, and the Pakistan-China Pipeline. The Kazakhstan-China Pipeline was completed in 2006 and runs approximately 1200 kilometers from Atusu, Kazakhstan to Dushanzi, China, which is a western distribution center and strategic petroleum reserve site. While the pipelines capacity is approximately 200,000 bbl/d, China imported an average of only 100,000 bbl/d in 2008.[96] This underutilization was due to pricing disputes and lack of supply in Russia, not a lack of demand in China.

Illustration 6. China's External Pipelines

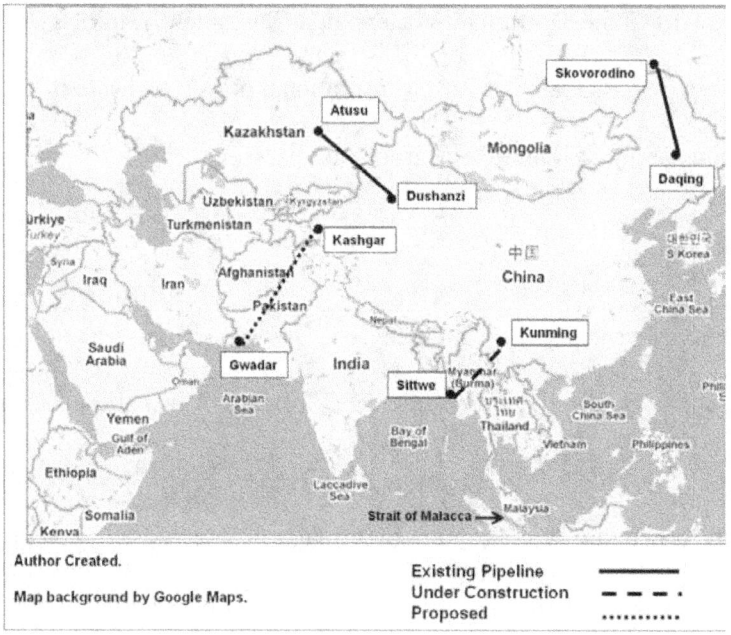

The East Siberian-Pacific Ocean (ESPO) Pipeline Spur runs approximately 1,000 kilometers from Skovorodino in Russia to Daqing, China. The CNPC financed the building of the spur at a cost of approximately $436 million.[97] This is a large but worthwhile investment, as it costs approximately twice as much to import oil from Russia via railroad vice the pipeline.[98] Russian and Chinese officials announced on September 27, 2010 that the pipeline spur would

---

[96] Andrew Erikson and Gabriel B. Collins, "China's Oil Security Pipe Dream: The Reality, and Strategic Consequences, of Seaborne Imports," *Naval War College Review*, Naval War College, Newport (2010): 94.

[97] Erikson and Collins, 96.

[98] Ibid.

begin delivering 300,000 bbl/d to China on January 1, 2011.[99] Testing of the pipeline will begin in October 2010, with small volumes of oil being pushed thru the system starting in November.[100] The terminus of the pipeline being at Daqing is advantageous to the Chinese, because Daqing is a primary distribution and refinery facility as well as a strategic petroleum reserve site.

The CNPC announced on September 11, 2010 that it has begun construction of the Myanmar-China Pipeline and a refinery at the pipeline's terminus in Yunnan Provence. Development of the Myanmar-China Pipeline began in 2004 when Yunnan University professor Yang Xiaohui publically stated the need for a pipeline from Myanmar to China as a means to bypass the Strait of Malacca.[101] The pipeline will run from Sittwe, Myanmar, on the Indian Ocean, to Kunming, China and will deliver approximately 12 billion cubic meters of oil a year to China.[102] Oil tankers from the Middle East or Africa will be able to dock and download their oil at Sittwe, versus passing through the Strait of Malacca in route to China. The CNPC plans to build port facilities at Sittwe "capable of berthing tankers of 300,000 deadweight tonnage, as well as storage facilities capable of holding more than four million barrels of crude."[103] The completion of the Myanmar-China Pipeline and associated refinery will give China an alternate delivery route for Middle Eastern and African shipments and another strategic petroleum reserve

---

[99] Yahoo, "Russia Prepares to Open Oil Pipeline to China," September 27, 2010, http://in news.yahoo.com/137/20100927/760/twl-russia-prepares-to-open-oil-pipeline.html (accessed September 28, 2010).

[100] Ibid.

[101] Erikson and Collins, 98.

[102] Winnie Zhu, "CNPC Starts Building China Part of Myanmar Pipelines, Yunnan Oil Refinery," *Bloomberg News*, September 12, 2010, http://www.bloomberg.com/news/2010-09-13/cnpc-starts-building-china-part-of-myanmar-pipelines-update1- html (accessed September 14, 2010).

[103] Erikson and Collins, 98.

site. Delivering oil to Yunnan via the Myanmar-China Pipeline may also lower energy costs in Yunnan, as Yunnan currently receives its petroleum products from the distant east coast.

The Pakistan-China Pipeline continues to be an on again-off again venture. A pipeline between Pakistan and China would offer China several advantages, but there are significant challenges keeping the pipeline from becoming reality. For China, the advantages are another overland energy transport system that bypasses the Strait of Malacca, as well as opens the possibility of linking into Iranian oil directly via a pipeline spur. A Pakistan-China Pipeline would likely begin at Gwadar, Pakistan and run north into China's Xinjiang Provence. Gwadar is a likely starting point for the pipeline as China has invested heavily in the port facilities there and has an established presence. There are multiple challenges associated with a Pakistan-China Pipeline, and these challenges will likely halt any further progress for the next several years. First, amongst the challenges is the volatile security environment in Pakistan. China is hesitant to invest millions of dollars in a project that is difficult to secure and could be damaged either directly by insurgents or indirectly by Pakistani counterinsurgency operations. Second, are the geographical challenges. A Pakistan-China Pipeline is more ambitious from an engineering perspective than even the Alaskan Pipeline, which is an engineering marvel. The Pipeline would "need to lift oil from sea level at Gwadar up to the 15,400-foot-high Khunjerab Pass, requiring massive pumping power and steady electrical supplies in remote areas…. By way of comparison, the Trans-Alaska and Baku–Tbilisi–Ceyhan pipelines climb from sea level to apogees of 2,800 feet and 9,000 feet, respectively, before returning to sea level."[104] China has weighed the costs and benefits of a Pakistan-China pipeline, and for the time being, has passed on the project.

---

[104] Erikson and Collins, 102.

China sees external pipelines as a means to diversify its access channels, but some analysts argue that pipelines are the wrong strategy. Andrew Erickson and Gabriel Collins argue in *Naval War College Review* that seaborne shipments remain the safest and most flexible means of oil importation, and that "pipelines are not likely to increase Chinese oil import security in quantitative terms, because the additional volumes they bring in will be overwhelmed by China's demand growth; the country's net reliance on seaborne oil imports will grow over time, pipelines notwithstanding."[105] They state that while the Kazakhstan and ESPO pipelines are good investments, pipelines through Burma and Pakistan are not. Erickson and Collins see these pipelines as unsound because they still require oil shipments to initially travel via ship, are excessively costly (versus shipping), and the security environments in Myanmar and Pakistan are not conducive to long vulnerable pipelines.[106] Erickson and Collins' points are valid, especially concerning security in Pakistan, but they fail to consider the fact that Myanmar is one of the world's largest natural gas producers and the Myanmar-China Pipeline will transport not only oil, but also natural gas. This makes the Myanmar-China Pipeline an extremely lucrative project for the Chinese.

---

[105] Ibid., 91.

[106] Ibid.

Natural Gas

Iran

In June of 2009, China reached an agreement with Iran for CNPC to develop the South Pars natural gas field. The South Pars field is an extension of Qatar's North Field.[107] The South Pars field contains an estimated 436 billion cubic feet of gas and accounts for 60 percent of Iran's and 10 percent of the world's gas reserves.[108] By controlling the development of the South Pars field China will have access to steady supplies of natural gas for years to come.

China and Iran's increasing interconnectedness will continue to influence China's foreign policy. The more China depends on Iran for resources, the less likely she will be to support United States initiatives to curtail Iranian influence or arms development. China hopes to maintain close ties to Iran without unnecessarily provoking the United States. According to Shi Yinhong, an analyst at the People's University in Beijing, believes that, "China will do its utmost to find a balance"[109] in its dealings with the United States and Iran. China, as a United Nations Security Council member, can veto proposals the United States or any member brings against Iran. Instead of a direct veto, China can also dilute security resolutions to such an extent that they are virtually meaningless. This has been extremely frustrating to the United States, especially as she attempts to garner international support for sanctions against Iran for failing to be forthcoming about its nuclear programs. Many analysts believe it will be difficult to, "push

---

[107] Offshore-Technology, "South Pars, Qatar North Field, Iran," http://www.offshore-technology.com/projects/southpars/ (accessed October 5, 2010).

[108] Ibid.

[109] Michael Wines, "China's Ties with Iran Complicate Diplomacy," *New York Times,* September 29, 2009, http://www.nytimes.com/2009/09/30/world/asia/30china.html?_r=1(accessed October 5, 2010).

44

meaningful sanctions against Iran through the United Nations Security Council (UNSC), where China not only holds a veto but has also been one of Iran's more reliable defenders."[110]

Myanmar

China's agreements with Myanmar concerning the Myanmar-China Pipeline have ensured China access to a steady supply of natural gas for years to come. Myanmar has an estimated 21 trillion cubic feet of natural gas reserves and they have agreed to supply China with natural gas until 2042.[111] Myanmar is Asia's fourth largest natural gas producer with production reaching 11.5 billion cubic meters in 2009.[112] Myanmar's military government is looking to increase natural gas exportation to stimulate its economy and ensure it remains in power. The ruling military junta sees China as the perfect choice with which to partner economically and politically and will go to great measures to remain on good terms with China. This includes preferential access to Myanmar's resources in return for Chinese economic assistance and political top cover.

China's interaction with Myanmar highlights its pragmatic worldview. China is willing to collaborate with a military dictatorship, regardless of world opinion, so long as it serves their interests. In fact, China used its United Nations Security Council veto power in January 2007 to block a UNSC resolution criticizing Myanmar's military junta in order to gain access to Myanmar

---

[110] Ibid.

[111] Irvin, Sherry, "Myanmar Natural Gas to Supply China," http://www.enerlix.com/environmental-technology/article_3095 htm (accessed October 5, 2010).

[112] Winnie Zhu, "CNPC Starts Building China Part of Myanmar Pipelines, Yunnan Oil Refinery," *Bloomberg News*. September 12, 2010, http://www.bloomberg.com/news/2010-09-13/cnpc-starts-building-china-part-of-myanmar-pipelines-update1- html (accessed September 14, 2010).

resources.[113] China additionally leveraged its diplomatic and economic powers to influence Myanmar by promising to build spurs off the Myanmar-China Pipeline to provide gas to Myanmar's populace and economic sector.[114]

Other Significant Natural Resources

China needs minerals and metals to fuel its industry and drive its economy. Three of the most important items it needs are cobalt, copper and lithium. Cobalt is used in the computer industry and to make temperature and stress resistant alloys. Copper is used in myriad industrial applications, and lithium is essential to the production of electronic items, and lithium ion batteries. As electronic items become even more prolific in the 21st century, access to lithium, to make and run electronic equipment will be crucial to China. While China is pursuing cobalt, copper and lithium around the globe, this section will focus on China's activities in the Democratic Republic of the Congo (DRC) and Afghanistan.

Democratic Republic of the Congo

China had limited dealings with the DRC until 2007 when the two reached an agreement where China would offer $8 billion in developmental aid in exchange for DRC resources.[115] These resources primarily include cobalt and copper. The DRC holds 40 percent of the world's cobalt reserves, as well as significant amounts of copper. [116] The $8 billion aid package consists

---

[113] Energy Tribune, "Myanmar Natural Gas Going to China," *Energy Tribune*. June 12, 2007, http://www.energytribune.com/articles.cfm?aid=515&idli=3 (accessed October 5, 2010).

[114] Ibid.

[115] Ampiah and Naidu, 98.

[116] Ibid.

of two parts. In one part, China's state owned Exim Bank would loan $3 billion to the DRC for mining development. In the second part, the Chinese state owned China Railway Engineering Company and Sinohydro would complete $5 billon in infrastructure projects.[117] These infrastructure projects include a 3,200 km railroad, a 3,200 km road, power lines, power plants, water distribution, dams, 30 hospitals, 145 health centers, 4 universities and tens of thousands of houses.[118] While these infrastructure improvements and associated jobs will improve the quality of life of local Congolese, the Chinese are not doing this for humanitarian reasons, but to exploit resources.

In return for the developmental aid, the DRC agreed to join the Chinese in creating a joint mining company known as Socomin, with its headquarters in Beijing.[119] China will control 62 percent of Socomin, with a Congolese company holding the remaining 32 percent. In agreeing to the $8 billion in aid, the DRC has effectively given China control of both its natural resources and almost half of the world's cobalt supply. While China undoubtedly sees this as a good deal, ironically so do the Congolese, at least for now.

The DRC has had difficulty obtaining aid from the International Monetary Fund and World Bank due to corruption and transparency issues. In opening their doors to China, the DRC is able to secure funds that make immediate improvements in the lives of the people without the Western requirement of governmental improvements. The $8 billion in loans provided to the

---

[117] Ibid.

[118] Ibid.

[119] Ibid.

DRC is equivalent to almost three times the DRC's annual budget.[120] This much-needed influx of funds will allow the DRC government to begin rebuilding after years of war. However not all Congolese agreed with the deal struck with China, no matter how much they needed outside support. When the DRC government announced the deal at Parliament in May of 2008, 150 members of the opposition party walked out.[121] They were protesting the fact that China stands to gain the most from the development of the DRC's resources. China is estimated to make $80 billion in profits for their $8 billion investment, while the DRC is estimated to only gain $40 billion in profits.[122] Discussions of profit aside, the DRC is currently rebuilding its infrastructure and in addition to economic aid, China has sent its military to assist in reconstruction.

China, in an effort to be seen as a responsible world leader and help secure its investments, offered soldiers to the United Nations Mission in the Democratic Republic of Congo (MONUC) beginning in 2003. These troops typically include engineers and medical personnel, and the people of the DRC reportedly appreciate their presence. At an awards ceremony for the Chinese soldiers in 2009 a DRC official stated. "The Chinese peacekeeping troops improved the road infrastructure and medical condition in south Kivu area with their practical actions. Today's ceremony is an encouragement for your professional dedication, spirit of humanism, spirit of perseverance and strict discipline."[123] The Chinese soldiers have been able to advance CCP goals

---

[120] Hannah Edinger and Johanna Jansson, "China Stirs the DRC Financing Pot," September 12, 2008, http://www.miningweekly.com/article/china-stirs-the-drc-financing-pot-2008-09-12 (accessed October 17, 2010).

[121] Ibid.

[122] Ibid.

[123] Xu Feng and Wu Guoqiang, "Chinese Peacekeepers to Congo (K) Receive UN Medals," June 9, 2009, http://english.chinamil.com.cn/site2/special-reports/2009-06/09/content_1801901.htm (accessed October 16, 2010).

in the DRC by building infrastructure and establishing rapport with the local Congolese through medical services.

China has successfully gained access to nearly half of the world's cobalt supply and vast deposits of copper and other minerals through the combined use of her elements of national power. Through diplomacy, China was able to broker the aid for resources deal that gained her access to the DRC's resources. Operating through her state owned enterprises, China was able to provide the $8 billion in economic aid need to secure the agreement and by employing its military China is able to improve required infrastructure, build goodwill and secure its investments at low cost. China's actions in the DRC are an excellent example of a nation using its elements of national power to achieve its objectives.

Afghanistan

Afghanistan is a dangerous and chaotic place, but China sees opportunity there. China has shown that she is not afraid to invest in unstable environments if she believes the potential gains outweigh the risk. Chinese businesses began operating in Afghanistan shortly after the United States' initial combat operations in 2001.[124] Since then they have continued to expand their presence throughout Afghanistan. The most substantial Chinese investment to date in Afghanistan is with the Aynak copper mine in Logar province. The Aynak site was discovered in

---

[124] Aziz, Huq, "Chinese Takeout," *Foreign Policy*, June 15, 2010, http://www.foreignpolicy.com/articles/2010/06/15/chinese_takeout?print=yes&hidecomments=yes&page=f ull[7/19/2010 (accessed July 28, 2010).

1974 by a combined Afghan and Soviet team, but it was never developed due to the war.[125]

Anyak is estimated to hold 240 trillion tons of copper and China's Metallurgical Construction

Corporation (MCC) won the $3 billion deal to develop the site in the spring of 2009.[126]

Metallurgical Construction Corporation's winning of the contract instigated some controversy.

Several western companies believe that MCC won the contract only after bribing an Afghan

official with $20 million.[127] These charges were never substantiated, and MCC continues its plan

for development. As part of the deal, MCC/China agreed to make substantial infrastructure

improvements in Afghanistan. These improvements include "an onsite copper smelter, a $500

million generating station to power the project and augment Kabul's electricity supply, a coal

mine to fuel the power station, a groundwater system, roads, new homes, hospitals and schools

for mine workers and their families, and a railway line from the country's northern border with

Uzbekistan to its southeastern border with Pakistan."[128] It may be several years before China sees

a return on this investment. The austere environment and current security situation make

developing the site, and emplacing the associated infrastructure, extremely challenging. For the

time being, China appears willing to accomplish what it can, while 'free riding' off security

provided by the United States and its coalition partners.

---

[125] Jonathan S Landay, "China's Thirst for Copper Could Hold Key to Afghanistan's Future," *McClatchy Newspaper*, March 8, 2009, http://www.mcclatchydc.com/2009/03/08/63452/chinas-thirst-for-copper-could html#ixzz11WR2k1hO (accessed October 5, 2010).

[126] Ibid.

[127] Jalinek, Paulin, "Afghan Official Said to Take Bribe for Copper Deal," *USA Today*, November 18, 2009, http://www.usatoday.com/news/world/2009-11-18-afghanistan-bribe_N htm (accessed July 21, 2010).

[128] Landay.

China's acquisition of the Aynak mine was a major coup, but that may just be the beginning of large-scale Chinese investment in Afghanistan. In the summer of 2010, a United States-led geological team released a report assessing that Afghanistan had an estimated $1trillion in untapped natural resources.[129] The lithium reserves are so vast that they may make Afghanistan the "Saudi Arabia of lithium".[130] While many countries, including the United States, will jockey for access to these resources, Aziz Huq believes that the "real winner from new natural-resource wealth beyond the Khyber Pass will be China."[131] This is because China is willing to accept risk, can underbid competitors, is able to directly tie business contracts to developmental aid and its companies are not above bribery to achieve objectives.[132] Although China is satisfied with letting the United States and its partners bear the burden in Afghanistan, she is understands that a stable Afghanistan is in her best interest. To this end China will continue to influence the Afghan and Pakistani governments through diplomacy and economics to establish conditions that are favorable to her.

Conclusion

China has secured reliable access to resources by maximizing production of its domestic sources and diversifying its foreign sources. In dealing with foreign countries, China has masterfully employed the elements of national power to gain and maintain access to resources. A steady resource supply will enable China to continue its economic growth, placate its growing

---

[129] James Risen, "U.S. Identifies Vast Mineral Riches in Afghanistan," *The New York Times*, June 13, 2010, http://www.nytimes.com/2010/06/14/world/asia/14minerals.htm (accessed July 28, 2010).

[130] Ibid.

[131] Huq.

[132] Ibid.

population and expand its influence. China has addressed all of the options outlined by the IEA for meeting its energy and resource needs. The International Energy Agency (IEA) describes China's options for ensuring energy security as "developing domestic resources to the maximum possible, creating strategic reserves, seeking foreign technology and investment, establishing reliable and secure oil trading channels, and making strategic investments in upstream production facilities abroad".[133]

China has restructured its energy sector and invested heavily in technology in an effort to get the most out of its domestic resources. She is well underway in her effort to establish a strategic oil reserve, and she has spread these reserves across the country to enable distribution and limit risk. China has realized that she needs innovative technology to solve some of her resource problems and has opened her doors to increased foreign investment and energy partnership. She has completed the construction of two external oil pipelines, is in the process of constructing a third and has instituted the 'string of pearls' strategy to ensure steady and reliable access to foreign sources. Finally, she has used all elements of her national power to secure access to vast amounts of resources in foreign countries.

China's resource security affects U.S. policy primarily in three ways. First, a resource secure China is difficult to leverage or threaten. China, by establishing a multifaceted supply approach, has mitigated the creation of a single critical source of supply that the United States could target. Attempts to disrupt the flow of foreign shipments at sea will be dangerous due to China's increasing naval presence in the South Pacific and Indian Ocean (string of pearls), and China will still have significant domestic supplies and access to resources in Russia, even if

---

[133] International Energy Agency, "China's Worldwide Quest for Energy Security,".

routes from the Middle East and/or Africa were interdicted. Additionally, it is politically dangerous, and most likely ineffective in any case, to threaten sanctions against China with American energy companies so deeply integrated into China's resource development structure. China, secure in the knowledge that her natural resource demands can be meet even with potential disruptions abroad, is poised to resist pressure from the United States or the International Community.

Second, since China's resource security depends to a large degree on foreign supply, it will be challenging for the United States to pressure countries with which China has resource ties. China is a pragmatist and is willing to work with pariah states to meet its resource demands. China has shown in the past that she is willing to oppose or veto United Nations actions against her partner states. Iran is one example of China protecting a resource partner state. While China has agreed to sanctions against Iran, she has seen that these sanctions are not as restrictive as the United States would like. China's membership on the United Nations Security Council ensures that she will generally be able protect one of her partner states against concerted negative international action.

Myanmar is another example of China using its position on the Security Council to protect a partner. China effectively opposed Myanmar's addition to the United Nations' permanent agenda (addition to the permanent agenda allows for a continual review of Myanmar and its ruling military junta, thus setting the conditions for future United Nations actions against the junta) until 2006, when nine of the fifteen members voted for Myanmar's inclusion.[134] China

---

[134] R Hariharan, "Myanmar: U.N. Security Council's Move to Tackle the Military Regime," http://www.saag.org/common/uploaded_files/paper1955.html (accessed October 19, 2010).

even went as far as to block pressure on Myanmar to allow international aid into the country after a tsunami killed thousands in 2008 in an effort to keep foreigners from entering the country and seeing firsthand the effects of oppressive military rule.[135]

Third, China's increasing influence in developing areas will cause the United States to revisit its foreign engagement policies. A prime example is Africa. With China expanding its influence and presence in Africa, the United States needs to re-examine the degree to which it will engage African nations. The United States has taken a major step forward in standing up U.S. Africa Command to plan and synchronize U.S. engagements on the continent. However, with increased American presence comes the possibility of increased conflict or competition between the United States and China. The United States needs to carefully consider its actions in Africa so that it can increase its influence and access while at the same time appearing not to threaten China's access to precious resources.

China is not currently a direct threat to the United States' security, but her growing stature and influence makes her a fierce competitor on the global stage. Competition between the United States and China will increase as resources diminish. Competition is the natural state between the two nations, but conflict does not have to be. It is in the best interest of China and the United States to reach a balanced accommodation and to work together in enabling global stability.

---

[135] Earthtimes, "Rights Group Slams Indonesia, China for Protecting Myanmar Junta," http://www.earthtimes.org/articles/news/204519,rights-group-slams-indonesia-china-for-protecting-myanmar-junta.html (accessed October 19, 2010).

BIBLIOGRAPHY

Books

Ampiah, Kweku and Sanusha Naidu, eds. *Crouching Tiger, Hidden Dragon? Africa and China.* Scottsville: University of KwaZulu-Natal Press, 2008.

Kynge, James. *China Shakes The World.* London: Phoenix, 2007.

Zweig, David. *Internationalizing China: Domestic Interests and Global Linkage.* Ithaca: Cornell University Press, 2002.

Articles

Alami, Faycal. "Chinese Policy in Africa: Stakes, Strategy and Implications." Strategy Research Project, U.S. Army War College, Carlisle Barracks (2008).

Bolt, Paul J. and Adam K. Gray. "China's National Security Strategy." United States Air Force Academy, Colorado Springs (2007).

Butts, Kent H. and Brent Bankus. "China's Pursuit of Africa's Natural Resources." Center for Strategic Leadership, U.S. Army War College, Carlisle Barracks (2009).

Downs, Erika S. "China's "New" Energy Administration." *China Business Review* (November/December 2008): 42-45.

Erikson, Andrew and Gabriel B. Collins. "China's Oil Security Pipe Dream: The Reality, and Strategic Consequences, of Seaborne Imports." *Naval War College Review*, Naval War College, Newport (2010).

Hurst, Cindy. "China's Oil Rush in Africa." Institute for the Analysis of Global Security; Foreign Military Studies Office, Fort Leavenworth: United States Training and Doctrine Command (2006).

Kaplan, Robert D. "The Geography of Chinese Power: How Far Can Beijing Reach on Land and at Sea?" *Foreign Affairs* 89, no. 3, (May/June 2010): 22-41.

Lee, Stacy L. "China's Energy Security: The Grand "Hedging" Strategy." Monograph, School of Advanced Military Studies, Fort Leavenworth: United States Army Command and General Staff College (2010).

Parenti, Jennifer L. "China-Africa Relations in the 21st Century." *Joint Forces Quarterly*, issue 52 (1st quarter, 2009):118-124.

Rogers, Philippe D. "Dragon with a Heart of Darkness? Countering Chinese Influence in Africa." *Joint Forces Quarterly* 47, 4th Quarter (2007).

Taylor, Ian. "China's Foreign Policy towards Africa in the 1990s." *The Journal of Modern African Studies* 36, no. 3 (Sep 1998): 443-460.

Mearsheimer, John J. "China's Unpeaceful Rise." *Current History* 105, no. 165 (April 2006): 160-162.

Electronic Documents

"Angola Mulls Chinese Military Deals." *AFP*. May 28, 2010. http://www.google.com/hostednews/afp/article/ALeqM5gmU9VQ_xDYErwwsGwR1snJ Pe4Lug (accessed October 16, 2010).

Baldauf, Scott. "China, Eager for Oil, Expands Investment in Nigeria and Guinea." *Christian Science Monitor*. October 30, 2009. http://www.csmonitor.com/World/Africa/2009/1030/p06s04-woaf.html (accessed October 16, 2010).

Barchfield, Jenny. "China Bests US as World's Top Energy User." *The Boston Globe*. July 21, 2010. http://www.boston.com/news/science/articles/2010/07/21/china_bests_us_as_worlds_top_energy_user/ (accessed July 21, 2010).

Britannica Online Encyclopedia. "Strait of Malacca." http://www.britannica.com/EBchecked/topic/359411/Strait-of-Malacca (accessed August 3, 2010).

Buckley, Chris and Lucy Hornby. "China Defends Export Policies Against WTO Complaint." *Reuters*. June 24, 2009. http://www.reuters.com/article/idUSBJC00034320090624 (accessed July 21, 2010).

Butts Kent and Brent Bankus. "China's Pursuit of Africa's Natural Resources." Center for Strategic Leadership, June 2009. http://www.dean.usma.edu/departments/geo/Geog/Publications/Understanding%20Africa.pdf (accessed July 28, 2010).

Central Intelligence Agency. "The World Fact Book: China." https://www.cia.gov/library/publications/the-world-factbook/geos/ch.html (accessed July 21, 2010).

Chen, Xavier. "Developing China's Natural Gas Market: The Energy Policy Challenges." *International Energy Agency*. 2002. http://www.iea.org/textbase/nppdf/free/2000/chinagas2002.pdf (accessed September 16, 2010).

"China's Energy Conditions and Policies." 2008. http://www.china.org.cn/e-white/index.htm (accessed July 21, 2010).

"China's National Defense in 2008." http://www.china.org.cn/government/central_government/2009-01/20/content_17155577.htm (accessed October 16, 2010).

"China's Policy on Natural Resources." December 2003. http://www.china.org.cn/e-white/index.htm (accessed July 21, 2010).

"China Tarim Oilfield Aims at 50mln tonnes of Oil, Gas Output in 2020". *Xinhua News Agency*. April 3, 2009. http://www.highbeam.com/doc/1P2-20095945.html (accessed September 6, 2010).

CNPC, "Daqing Oil Province." http://www.cnpc.com.cn/en/aboutcnpc/ourbusinesses/explorationproduction/operatediol/default.htm (accessed September 4, 2010).

Devonshire-Ellis, Chris. "China's String of Pearls Strategy." *China Briefing*, March 18, 2009. http://www.china-briefing.com/news/2009/03/18/china%e2%80%99s-string-of-pearls-strategy.html (accessed August 3, 2010).

Edinger, Hannah and Johanna Jansson. "China stirs the DRC financing pot." September 12, 2008. http://www.miningweekly.com/article/china-stirs-the-drc-financing-pot-2008-09-12 (accessed October 17, 2010).

Encarta Online Dictionary. "Natural Resources."
http://encarta.msn.com/dictionary_1861696711/natural_resource.html (accessed August 3, 2010).

Encarta Online Dictionary. "Security."
http://encarta.msn.com/encnet/features/dictionary/DictionaryResults.aspx?lextype=3&search=security (accessed August 3, 2010).

Energy Information Administration. "China Country Analysis." July 2009. Energy Information Agency. Department of Energy. Washington, D.C.: DOE, 2009.
http://www.eia.doe.gov/emeu/cabs/China/Background.html (accessed July 28, 2010).

_____. "World Oil Transit Chokepoints." Energy Information Agency. Department of Energy. Washington, D.C.: DOE, 2008.
http://www.eia.doe.gov/emeu/cabs/World_Oil_Transit_Chokepoints/Background.html (accessed July 28, 2010).

Earth Times. "Rights Group Slams Indonesia, China for Protecting Myanmar Junta."
http://www.earthtimes.org/articles/news/204519,rights-group-slams-indonesia-china-for-protecting-myanmar-junta.html (accessed October 19, 2010).

Feng, Xu and Wu Guoqiang. "Chinese Peacekeepers to Congo (K) Receive UN Medals." June 9, 2009. http://english.chinamil.com.cn/site2/special-reports/2009-06/09/content_1801901.htm (accessed October 16, 2010).

Ferguson, Niall. "Hegemony or Empire?".*Foreign Affairs*. September/October 2003.
http://www.foreignaffairs.com/articles/59200/niall-ferguson/hegemony-or-empire?page=2 (accessed October 14, 2010).

Goodman. Peter S. "China Rushes Towards Oil Pact with Iran." *Washington Post*. February 18, 2006. http://www.washingtonpost.com/wp-dyn/content/article/2006/02/17/AR2006021702146.html (accessed September 23, 2010).

Hare, Paul. "China in Angola: An Emerging Energy Partnership." May 9, 2007.
http://www.jamestown.org/programs/chinabrief/single/?tx_ttnews%5Btt_news%5D=3997&tx_ttnews%5BbackPid%5D=196&no_cache=1 (accessed October 16, 2010).

Hariharan, R. "Myanmar: U.N. Security Council's Move to Tackle the Military Regime."
http://www.saag.org/common/uploaded_files/paper1955.html (accessed October 19, 2010).

Hoven, Michael. "Chinese Legislators Want Increased Strategic Oil Reserves." March 8, 2010.
http://www.heatingoil.com/blog/chinese-legislators-want-increased-strategic-oil-reserves308/ (accessed September 16, 2010).

Huq, Aziz. "Chinese Takeout." *Foreign Policy,* June 15, 2010.
http://www.foreignpolicy.com/articles/2010/06/15/chinese_takeout?print=yes&hidecomments=yes&page=full[7/19/2010 (accessed July 28, 2010).

"Interpreting China's Grand Strategy." *RAND*. 2000.
http://www.rand.org/pubs/research_briefs/RB61/index1.html (accessed September 14, 2010).

International Energy Agency. "China's Worldwide Quest for Energy Security." 2000.
http://www.iea.org/textbase/nppdf/free/2000/china2000.pdf (accessed August 3, 2010).

Investorwords.com. "Natural Resources."
http://www.investorwords.com/3210/natural_resources.html (accessed August 3, 2010).

Irvin, Sherry. "Myanmar Natural Gas to Supply China." http://www.enerlix.com/environmental-technology/article_3095.htm (accessed October 5, 2010).

Jalinek, Paulin. "Afghan Official Said to Take Bribe for Copper Deal." *USA Today*. November 18, 2009. http://www.usatoday.com/news/world/2009-11-18-afghanistan-bribe_N.htm (accessed July 21, 2010).

Janes, "Sentinel Country Risk Assessment." *Jane's*. http://www4.janes.com/subscribe/sentinel/CNAS_doc_view.jsp?Sent_Country=China&Prod_Name=CNAS&K2DocKey=/content1/janesdata/sent/cnasu/chins040.htm@current (accessed July 28, 2010).

Kurtenbach, Elaine. "China's Sinopec, Iran ink Yadavaran Deal." *USA Today*, December 10, 2007. http://www.usatoday.com/money/economy/2007-12-09-231119728_x.htm (accessed September 30, 2010).

Landay, Jonathan S. "China's Thirst for Copper Could Hold Key to Afghanistan's Future." *McClatchy Newspaper*. March 8, 2009. http://www.mcclatchydc.com/2009/03/08/63452/chinas-thirst-for-copper-could.html#ixzz11WR2k1hO (accessed October 5, 2010).

Lee, Diana. "Pirates Strike at Will in the Straits of Malacca". *UNIORB*. May 1, 2005. http://uniorb.com/ATREND/piracy.htm (accessed August 3, 2010).

Lind, Michael. "For Liberal Internationalism." The Nation, (July 2009). http://www.newamerica.net/publications/articles/2007/liberal_internationalism_5538 (accessed November 19, 2010).

Mbendi, "China in Angola." http://www.mbendi.com/land/as/cj/p0025.htm (accessed October 16, 2010).

"Myanmar Natural Gas Going to China." *Energy Tribune*. June 12, 2007. http://www.energytribune.com/articles.cfm?aid=515&idli=3 (accessed October 5, 2010).

New World Encyclopedia. "Deng Xiaoping." http://www.newworldencyclopedia.org/entry/Deng_Xiaoping (accessed July 21, 2010).

Offshore Technology, "South Pars, Qatar North Field, Iran." http://www.offshore-technology.com/projects/southpars/ (accessed October 5, 2010).

Overhold. William H. "China and Globalization." May 19, 2005. http://www.rand.org/pubs/testimonies/2005/RAND_CT244.pdf (accessed September 21, 2010).

Peixin, Zha. "China and Globalization." October 10, 2003. http://www.chinese-embassy.org.uk/eng/dsjh/t27161.htm (accessed September 21, 2010).

Petersen, Alexondros. "Did China Just Win the Caspian Gas War?" *Foreign Policy*. July 1, 2010. http://www.foreignpolicy.com/articles/2010/07/07/did_china_just_win_the_caspian_gas_war (accessed August 31, 2010).

Risen, James. "U.S. Identifies Vast Mineral Riches in Afghanistan." *The New York Times*, June 13, 2010. http://www.nytimes.com/2010/06/14/world/asia/14minerals.htm (accessed July 28, 2010).

Ritchburg, Kieth B. "China Sentences American Geologist to 8 Years for Stealing State Secrets." *Washington Post*. July 25, 2010. http://www.washingtonpost.com/wp-dyn/content/article/2010/07/05/AR2010070500859.html?hpid=moreheadlines (accessed August 12, 2010).

"Russia Prepares to Open Oil Pipeline to China." September 27, 2010. http://in.news.yahoo.com/137/20100927/760/twl-russia-prepares-to-open-oil-pipeline.html (accessed September 28, 2010).

"Saudi Arabian Missiles." http://www.fas.org/irp/threat/missile/saudi.htm (accessed September 30, 2010).

Wines, Michael. "China's Ties with Iran Complicate Diplomacy." *New York Times.* September 29, 2009. http://www.nytimes.com/2009/09/30/world/asia/30china.html?_r=1(accessed October 5, 2010).

Yaqing, Qin. "China's Security Strategy with a Special Focus on East Asia." http://irchina.org/en/xueren/china/pdf/qyq2.pdf (accessed September 14, 2010).

Ying, Wang and Stephen Engle. "Pakistan Considers Building Gas Pipeline to China." April 22, 2009. http://www.bloomberg.com/apps/news?pid=email&sid=agFWKJ36isgg (accessed July 21, 2010).

Zhu, Winnie. "CNPC Starts Building China Part of Myanmar Pipelines, Yunnan Oil Refinery." *Bloomberg News.* September 12, 2010. http://www.bloomberg.com/news/2010-09-13/cnpc-starts-building-china-part-of-myanmar-pipelines-update1-.html (accessed September 14, 2010).

www.ingramcontent.com/pod-product-compliance
Lightning Source LLC
Chambersburg PA
CBHW082150290526
45794CB00008B/3240